DC COMICS

# BATMAN'S MISSIONS

Written by Beth Davies

**Editorial Assistant** Beth Davies
**Senior Editor** Hannah Dolan
**Designer** Thelma-Jane Robb
**Senior Designer** Nathan Martin
**Pre-Production Producer** Marc Staples
**Producer** Louise Daly
**Managing Editors** Elizabeth Dowsett, Simon Hugo
**Design Manager** Ron Stobbart
**Art Director** Lisa Lanzarini
**Publisher** Julie Ferris
**Publishing Director** Simon Beecroft

### Reading Consultant
Maureen Fernandes

First published in Great Britain in 2015 by Dorling Kindersley Limited
80 Strand, London, WC2R 0RL
A Penguin Random House Company

10 9 8 7 6 5 4 3 2 1
001–185650–Feb/15

Page design copyright © 2015 Dorling Kindersley Limited

A CIP catalogue record for this book
is available from the British Library.

ISBN: 978-0-24118-401-1

Colour reproduction by Altaimage, UK
Printed and bound in China by South China

**www.LEGO.com**
**www.dk.com**

A WORLD OF IDEAS:
**SEE ALL THERE IS TO KNOW**

# Contents

# Gotham City's Hero

Gotham City is a dark and dangerous place. The streets are filled with criminals and villains who want to cause trouble. The Gotham City Police Department struggles to keep them all under control. Luckily, the police have Batman to help them protect the city.

Batman wears a mask to hide his other identity – an important businessman named Bruce Wayne. Bruce loves Gotham City and vows to protect its citizens from crime. He does not have any superpowers, but he has trained very hard to increase his strength and become Batman. He has also built many tools to help him in his daring missions. Batman is the World's Greatest Detective.

# Robin

This is Robin, Batman's trusted sidekick and friend. He is very quick and agile. Batman is training Robin to be a great crime fighter, just like him. The brave duo have worked together on many difficult missions.

Batman has been teaching Robin martial arts, including stick-fighting. Robin uses his long stick to battle Batman's enemy, the Penguin. The Penguin's umbrella is no match for Robin's whirling stick!

# Meet the Gordons

Barbara Gordon works as a librarian during the day, but she transforms into an ace crime fighter named Batgirl at night. Batgirl battles baddies alongside Batman and Robin. She is both brave and intelligent. Her mask and Batsuit are similar to Batman's.

Commissioner James Gordon
is the chief police officer in Gotham
City. He is Barbara's father, but he
does not know she is secretly Batgirl.
Commissioner Gordon often calls on
Batman, Robin and Batgirl in times
of need. He shines a
bright Bat-Signal
into the night sky
when he needs
their help.

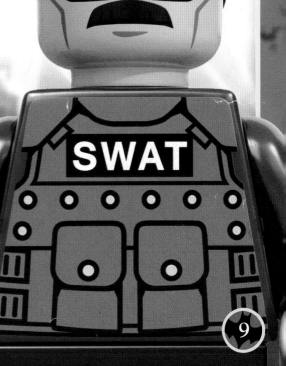

# The Joker

The Joker is a crazy criminal who loves to cause chaos in Gotham City. The Joker has a big smile, but he is not friendly. This colourful villain has many scary tricks up his purple sleeves.

The Joker often uses henchmen to carry out his plans. His horrible helper wears bright clown make-up to look like his boss.

The Joker is Batman's worst enemy. Batman has defeated the Joker many times. The Joker is now locked up in Arkham Asylum. He has to wear a bright orange prison uniform, which he thinks goes wonderfully with his bright green hair!

# Arkham Asylum

Arkham Asylum is a dark and spooky building on the edge of Gotham City. The Joker is locked up in Arkham Asylum as punishment for all the crimes he has committed. However, the Joker is not planning to stick around for long! He is plotting to break out of his cell in the middle of the night. Lots of other crazy criminals live in the cells of Arkham Asylum, too. Gotham City will be in big trouble if they are all plotting their escape.

# Arkham Escape

It is a normal night at Arkham Asylum. There is only one guard on duty, who watches over the inmates and patrols the building. When the guard checks on the Joker, the Joker tells him a hilarious joke. While the guard cries with laughter, the Joker slips past him and escapes!

Look out! The Joker has released
Scarecrow from his cell. Scarecrow
had been put in Arkham Asylum
as punishment for using a dangerous
gas that gives people bad dreams.
This villain's escape is Batman's
worst nightmare!

# Suiting Up

Bruce Wayne leaps into action when he hears about the trouble at Arkham Asylum. He must become Batman to save the day. Bruce rushes to prepare, but which Batsuit is right for the job?

This Batsuit has lots of strong armour. It is great for fighting super-strong enemies, but it is a little heavy.

Batman is hard to spot in this Arctic Batsuit, but only if he is on a mission somewhere snowy!

This Batsuit comes with a Bat-glider. It is useful if Batman needs to fly somewhere fast or track multiple enemies. Perfect!

# Villains on the Loose

Batman soars into the night sky wearing his Bat-glider. It is perfect for this mission. He can see all of Arkham Asylum. The villains are escaping in different directions! Robin rushes to battle Scarecrow and the Penguin on the ground. He battles them both using his amazing martial arts skills.

The Joker is too quick for the guard, but not for Batman! Batman swoops down from above to stop the Joker in his tracks! Batman and Robin capture the villains and Gotham City is safe once more. Good work!

# Bane

Batman does not have time to rest after his battle at Arkham Asylum! Another dangerous criminal is on the loose and only Batman can stop him. Bane is known for his huge muscles and incredible strength, but he also has a clever and devious mind.

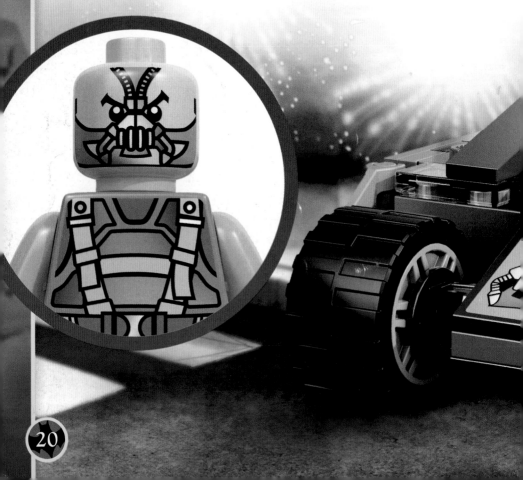

Bane's Tumbler car is tough and powerful. He uses it to race and smash through the streets of Gotham City. The vehicle has strong metal armour that protects Bane even if the car flips upside down.

# On the Move

Batman has many vehicles that help him fight crime. All of them are built in his favourite colour: black! His favourite car is called the Batmobile. Batman drives the Batmobile at top speeds to reach crime scenes around the city.

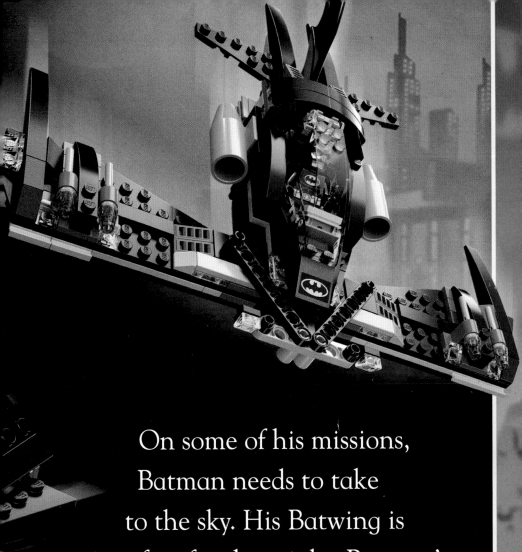

On some of his missions,
Batman needs to take
to the sky. His Batwing is
perfect for these jobs. Batman's
plane has two powerful jet
engines to help it speed through
the sky. Batman can also move
its huge wings forward and trap
his enemies between them.

# Batman vs Bane

Take cover! Batman pilots a huge flying machine called The Bat as he chases Bane across Gotham City. This mighty machine has two powerful engines that propel it through the air. It is also loaded with dangerous missiles and Batman is not afraid to use them!

Commissioner Gordon is tracking Bane on the ground. Batman must be careful not to hit his friend by mistake. Batman takes aim and fires! Bane's Tumbler screeches to a halt. When Bane leaps from the car, Commissioner Gordon arrests him.

# Crime-fighting Partners

Batman is always busy fighting crime in Gotham City. Every time he defeats a villain, another one appears with an even more evil scheme! Batman is sometimes called upon to help his fellow Super Heroes fight enemies around the world, too.

When Batman has to leave Gotham City, he asks Batgirl and Comissioner Gordon to watch over the city. He knows they won't let him – or Gotham City – down. Robin often joins him on his missions.

# Aquaman

One of Batman's Super Hero friends is named Aquaman. He lives deep under the sea. Aquaman is a powerful swimmer and can travel through the water at top speed. He can also breathe underwater.

Aquaman normally carries a special golden trident, but someone has stolen it!

Batman and Robin offer to use their famous detective skills to find the trident. They do not have Aquaman's underwater powers, so they need special gadgets for this mission.

Robin has a new scuba suit with large flippers to help him swim, and air tanks to help him survive underwater. His suit also has handy blue goggles.

# Black Manta

Ah ha! It's the evil Black Manta who has stolen Aquaman's trident and now he has captured Robin, too!

Robin does not like the robot shark Black Manta is using to guard his lair. The shark's mouth is full of sharp teeth and it has lasers attached to its sides.

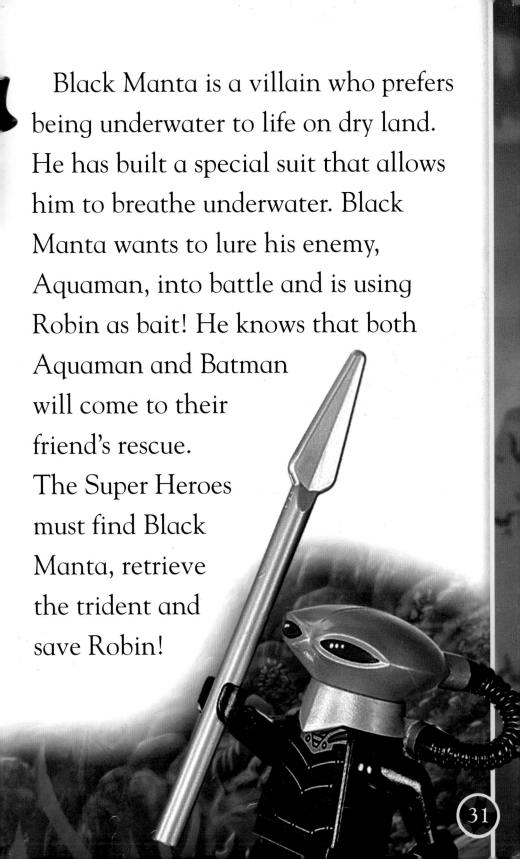

Black Manta is a villain who prefers being underwater to life on dry land. He has built a special suit that allows him to breathe underwater. Black Manta wants to lure his enemy, Aquaman, into battle and is using Robin as bait! He knows that both Aquaman and Batman will come to their friend's rescue. The Super Heroes must find Black Manta, retrieve the trident and save Robin!

# Rescue Robin!

In an emergency, nothing beats Batman's Batsub for undersea speed! Its sleek design helps Batman zoom through the water. The Batsub's computers find the quickest route to Black Manta's underwater temple lair. Batman and Aquaman race to rescue Robin.

Black Manta is waiting in his submarine, called the Sea Saucer. Aquaman quickly grabs his trident from the top of the temple and breaks Robin's chains. Working together, Batman and Aquaman soon disable the Sea Saucer and defeat Black Manta. Two Super Heroes are better than one!

# Green Lantern

Many of Batman's friends fight villains on Earth, but his friend Green Lantern defends the whole universe! He is part of a space police team called the Green Lantern Corps. Green Lantern has a power ring that gives him super-human abilities. He carries a large, green Power Battery to charge the ring.

Green Lantern's power ring allows him to create any object he can imagine. He has used the ring to build an awesome green spaceship, complete with green missiles. His creations are always green in colour!

Green Lantern is very powerful, as long as his power ring is charged. His only weakness is that any yellow-coloured objects drain his power, even bananas!

# Sinestro

Sinestro is an evil alien who used to be a loyal and courageous member of the Green Lantern Corps. He was banished from the team when he began to crave too much power. Now, he is Green Lantern's worst enemy. Sinestro carries yellow weapons that he knows will weaken Green Lantern.

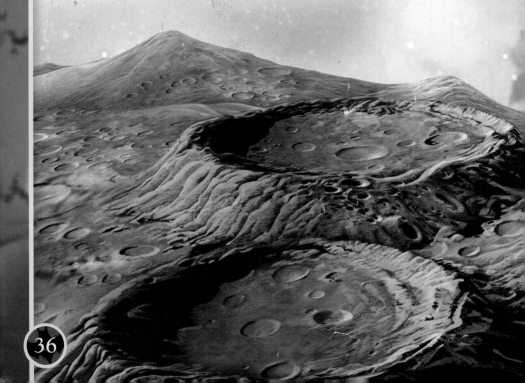

Sinestro has stolen the Power Battery that Green Lantern uses to charge his power ring, and locked it in a bright yellow cage! Green Lantern needs to rescue the Power Battery, but he grows weak when he gets close to the cage. Can Batman help him defeat Sinestro?

# Space Batman

Batman has built a special new Space Batsuit, so he can assist Green Lantern in his battle against Sinestro.

Batman's new Space Batsuit is fitted with all the high-tech gadgets Batman needs for his space mission. It has special technology and a mask to allow him to breathe in space. It also has his trusty Utility Belt, with all his best weapons attached. Finally, Batman's Batsuit has special mechanical wings that help him speed through outer space.

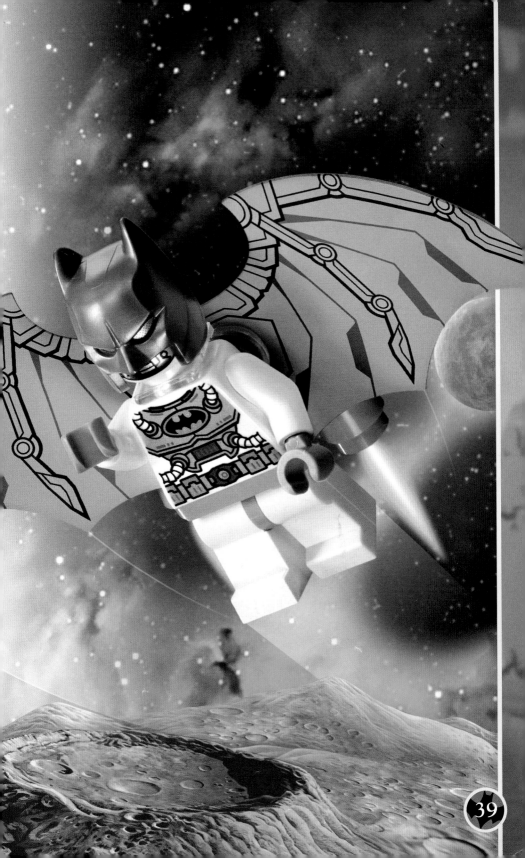

# Space Battle

Green Lantern is growing weaker
as his power ring's strength fades.
He cannot go near the yellow cage,
but he fires missiles at Sinestro from
his spaceship while Batman heads
for the imprisoned Power Battery.
Batman breaks into the cage using
a tool from his Utility Belt.

Batman returns the Power Battery to Green Lantern and in an instant his power is fully restored. Together, the heroes defeat Sinestro and lock him in his own yellow cage! Thanks to Batman and Green Lantern, the whole universe is safe once more.

# Ready for Anything

Batman is back in Gotham City. He has been very busy helping his fellow Super Heroes battle terrible foes. Together, they have defeated the villains and foiled their evil plans.

For now, Batman is happy to be back at home. He has more Batsuits to design, new vehicles to build and criminals to watch out for. When evil threatens, Batman is always prepared to leap into action and embark on his next important mission.

# Quiz

1. Who has Batman taught martial arts to?

2. What is Batgirl's other name?

3. What is James Gordon's job?

4. How do the police call Batman, Robin and Batgirl?

5. Where is the Joker locked away as punishment for his crimes?

6. Who drives an armoured Tumbler car?

7. What does Black Manta steal from Aquaman?

8. What colour weakens Green Lantern?

Answers on page 47.

# Glossary

**Agile**
able to move quickly and easily

**Banished**
sent away as punishment for bad behaviour

**Camouflaged**
coloured or patterned to blend in to the surrounding area

**Commissioner**
a senior police officer

**Corps**
a group of people doing a particular activity

**Crave**
to want something desperately

**Henchman**
a sidekick or helper

**Lure**
to tempt someone with something they want

**Martial arts**
various sports that can be used in self-defence or attack

**Meditation**
the practice of clearing or focusing the mind

**Scuba**
a device that allows the wearer to breathe underwater

**Toxic**
chemically dangerous or deadly

**Trident**
a three-pronged spear

**Vigilant**
aware and observant

# Index

---

**Answers to the quiz on pages 45 and 46:**
1. Robin 2. Barbara Gordon 3. Gotham City Police
Commissioner 4. They shine the Bat-Signal into the sky
5. Arkham Asylum 6. Bane 7. A golden trident 8. Yellow

# Have you read these other great books from DK?

**Snappy Crocodile Tale**
Follow Chris Croc's adventures from a baby
to mighty king of the river.

**Titanic**
This is the incredible true story of the
"unsinkable" ship that sank.

**LEGO® Legends of Chima™ The Race for CHI**
Jump into battle with the animal tribes
as they fight to win CHI.

**LEGO® *Star Wars*™ Return of the Jedi™**
Join Luke Skywalker as he helps the rebels
defeat the Empire.

**LEGO® Legends of Chima™ Heroes' Quest**
Meet the heroes of Chima™ and help them
find the Legend Beasts.

**LEGO® Legends of Chima™ Power Up!**
Discover the new tribes threatening Chima™
with their icy powers.